THOMAS DE QUI

¶ THOMAS DE QUINCEY was born in Manchester in 1785. He died in Edinburgh in 1859.

THOMAS DE QUINCEY
By courtesy of the Trustees of Dove Cottage and the Wordsworth Museum

THOMAS
DE QUINCEY

by

HUGH SYKES DAVIES

PUBLISHED FOR
THE BRITISH COUNCIL
BY LONGMAN GROUP LTD

LONGMAN GROUP LTD
Longman House, Burnt Mill, Harlow, Essex

*Associated companies, branches and
representatives throughout the world*

*First published 1964
Reprinted with minor amendments and
additions to the Bibliography 1972*

© Hugh Sykes Davies 1964, 1972

*Printed in Great Britain by
F. Mildner & Sons, London, EC1R 5EJ*

SBN 0 582 01167 1

DE QUINCEY

I

DE QUINCEY's best-known work, *Confessions of an English Opium-Eater*, was published in 1821, and it is characteristic of certain oddities in the pattern of his life and writings that both the date and the title give misleading impressions of his place in English literature. The date suggests that he was a Romantic of the second generation, to be placed with Byron, Shelley and Keats; but in fact he was thirty-six years old when he wrote the *Confessions*, and had been for the past twenty years an admirer and friend of Wordsworth and Coleridge. In literary taste and outlook, he belonged to the first generation of the English Romantics, not to the second. The title is no less misleading, with its suggestion of Byron and Keats, the sensational and the exotic; for the book itself is of a sobriety in subject and treatment which owed nothing to Byron or Keats, and much to Wordsworth.

The same date divides De Quincey's life into two parts almost equal in length, but in every other respect utterly different. Before it, he had written nothing; after it, he wrote the fourteen closely printed volumes which make up his collected works.[1] In the first part of his life, he moved in society, was the friend of literary men—the intimate friend of the greatest writers of his time. In the second part, he dropped out of all society, was cut off from all his friends, living almost as an exile from his own past. 'The years came', he wrote of his later life, '—for I have lived too long, reader, in relation to many things! and the report of me would

---

[1] The standard edition is that edited by D. Masson, 1889-90. Page references will be given as in this edition. They are often needed, because De Quincey rarely divided his long essays into sections or chapters which might be used to identify references.

have been better, or more uniform at least, had I died some twenty years ago—the years came in which circumstances made me an Opium-Eater; years through which a shadow as of sad eclipse sate and rested upon my faculties; years through which I was careless of all but those who lived within my inner circle, within "my heart of hearts".' In this second, eclipsed part of his life, he was almost entirely cut off from external experience, save that of writing for a living under a crushing weight of debt, and he came to depend, for mental and emotional sustenance, on his memories of the first and happier part. It was in this exploration of his own earlier life, in his study of the role of memory in the human personality, that he most closely resembled Wordsworth. And as the reader of Wordsworth's poetry finds himself inevitably involved in the events of his life, so the student of De Quincey's prose must become to some extent his biographer.

He was born in 1785, the second son of a Manchester merchant who died in 1793 after many years of ill-health, leaving a modest fortune to his widow and family. These were at once the happiest years of De Quincey's life, and also those, he came to believe, in which he had been marked out for ultimate misery. He was a small, gentle child, preferring the company of his sisters to that of his turbulent elder brother, and winning from them, rather than from his sternly dutiful mother, the warmth of affection which he so much needed. Their manner of life was peaceful, but rich in imagination. Like the Brontës a generation later, all the children of the family were writing long novels about elaborately conceived private worlds of their own. But this early happiness was broken up, first by the death of his most dearly loved sister, and then by the removal of the whole family after their father's death from their large house outside Manchester. Mrs De Quincey went to Bath, and it was there that she first sent Thomas to school. He showed at once a remarkable aptitude for Latin and Greek, and tasted the dangerous pleasure of being obviously the cleverest boy in a small school. After a short experience of a private school conducted by a clergyman, where he learnt nothing, but fortunately forgot nothing either, he was sent to Manchester Grammar School. From the point of view of his mother, and of the guardians appointed by his father's will, the choice was a good one. The school was then, as it is now, outstanding among the older Grammar Schools, and it had the further advantage that three years' study there would gain him an Exhibition to Oxford. But De Quincey disliked it from the first, for reasons which never emerge quite clearly, either from his long letters to his mother written at the time, or from the later accounts of his school life. There was hard work, but no question of ill-treatment, and in many ways he enjoyed special privileges. Perhaps the most persistent source of irritation was that his favourite exercise, walking, could only be indulged in through the streets of a city which showed, perhaps more clearly than any other place in Britain at that time, the immense brutalization of the physical conditions of life, and of intellectual and emotional standards, then being effected by the Industrial Revolution. In one of his letters to his mother, he wrote:

I am living in a town where the sole and universal object of pursuit is precisely that which I hold most in abhorrence. In this place trade is the religion, and money is the god. Every object I see reminds me of those occupations which run counter to the bent of my nature, every sentiment I hear sounds a discord to my own. I cannot stir out of doors but I am nosed by a factory, a cotton-bag, a cotton-dealer, or something else allied to that most detestable commerce. Such an object dissipates the whole train of romantic visions I had conjured up, and frequently gives the colouring to all my associations of ideas during the remainder of the day.[1]

It is easy to imagine with what force Wordsworth's *Lyrical Ballads* must have struck such a temperament, so situated. De Quincey seems to have read them in 1802, and at once

[1] Bairdsmith MSS, quoted in H. A. Eaton, *Thomas De Quincey* (1936), the most fully documented biography of De Quincey yet written.

became one of Wordsworth's earliest and most devoted disciples. They suggested to him the kind of life which he really wished to lead, and by contrast, brought his dislike of Manchester to a crisis. He fled from the school in the middle of the night, resolved never to return. It was the first of those flights from the stress of unpleasant realities which were to become a repeating pattern in his life, and its effect was to plunge him into difficulties in some ways greater than those he sought to escape.

His mother, deeply shocked by his rebellion, and fearing his influence upon her other children, agreed that he should set off on a walking tour. His first intention was to go to Wordsworth, with whom he was already in correspondence, but a kind of shyness overcame him, and instead of going to the Lakes, he went to North Wales. The allowance made to him was so small that he had to lodge in the humblest inns and farmhouses, and often he slept in the open, with no better shelter than a primitive tent, for which his walking stick served as a pole. As winter came on, this mode of life became impossible, but he was afraid to return home, lest he be sent back to Manchester. He fled again, breaking off all communication with his mother and guardians, resolved to lose himself in the anonymous vastness of London, and to live by borrowing money on the security of his expectations under his father's will. His negotiations with the moneylenders were tortuous, and ultimately unsuccessful, but they kept him in London for five months, in destitution and near-starvation, which nevertheless gained for him what was to prove more valuable than money—some of the most vivid and profound experiences of his early life.

Early in 1803, he seems to have received an assurance that he would not be sent back to Manchester, and he returned to his mother's home. Later in the year, he went up to Oxford, the poorer by the Exhibition which he might have had from Manchester Grammar School, and on an allowance which proved to be much too small. For the next five years, he kept his terms there, reading avidly within the official syllabus, especially in Latin and in Greek, but even more widely outside it, in German philosophy and above all in English literature. In 1808, he sat for his final examination, wrote a few papers which are said to have been brilliant, and then fled, as abruptly and more inexplicably than he had fled from school. Now, however, there was no question of returning home in disgrace. He was in possession of the small fortune left to him by his father, and he believed that it would be enough to enable him to lead the kind of life he had chosen for himself, that of a scholar and a gentleman, living in some remote and picturesque place, with a large library, and even larger but leisurely literary ambitions.

At Oxford, he seems to have had few friends, if any; perhaps there were few worth his making, for it was one of the less distinguished periods in the University's history. But he had made friends elsewhere, and distinguished ones. While still at Oxford, he had come to know Coleridge well, and soon after leaving it, he visited Wordsworth for the first time, though they had been in correspondence for some years. For several months, he lived at Dove Cottage with the Wordsworths, as an intimate friend, almost as a member of the family, and remained as tenant of the Cottage when they moved to a larger house nearby. For a few years, it seemed that he had succeeded in living the kind of life he had chosen, amid splendid scenery, in close friendship with the writer he admired above all others. But it was not to last. In 1813, De Quincey suffered an access of grief and illness, from which he sought relief in massive doses of laudanum. He had first became acquainted with the drug in London, in one of his vacations from Oxford, and had continued to use it—so he assures us—in moderation. But now it took hold of him with the ineluctable strength of an addiction, and the Grasmere idyll was over. His relations with Wordsworth and his family grew more distant—they had already seen what laudanum could do to a man, in the case of Coleridge. De Quincey himself grew irritable and touchy, resentful of their disapproval, and of what he took

—perhaps rightly—to be a certain loftiness in Wordsworth's attitude to him. Matters were made worse when he courted the daughter of a small farmer, and married her after she had borne him an illegitimate child. Dorothy Wordsworth, until now his intimate friend, thought the marriage unsuitable; though hardly a snob, she was sensitive to the special social hierarchy of the Lakes and its almost unique structure of peasants and small farmers. In a sense, De Quincey had let the gentry down by his marriage.

Worst of all, by ill-management and extravagance, above all in the purchase of books and in a generous but injudicious gift to Coleridge of several hundred pounds, the inheritance upon which De Quincey depended had been wasted away to almost nothing. Debts, bills and creditors crowded in on him, and the leisurely literary ambitions of his youth were transformed into an urgent need to write for ready money. In 1819 he went to Edinburgh, in a desperate and unsuccessful attempt to write for *Blackwood's Magazine*. In the following year he was in London, and by a great effort finished his first and perhaps his greatest work, the *Confessions*. Back at Grasmere, he and his family lived as if besieged—'shut up as usual', Dorothy Wordsworth wrote, 'the house always blinded—or left with but one eye to peep out of—he probably in bed—We hear nothing of him'.[1]

The first, and happier part, of De Quincey's life was at an end. From that time onward, his old friends 'heard nothing of him'. In 1825, his growing financial troubles drove him finally from Grasmere, from the last semblance of his life as a leisured scholar. He moved to Edinburgh, and became at last a contributor to *Blackwood's Magazine*, frequent, but not regular—regularity was, and always remained, beyond him. The next twenty years were spent there, or in Glasgow, hunted from one lodging to another by furious Scottish creditors, sometimes living with his family, but often alone, in hiding, without books, with

[1] Letter to Quillinan, 19 November 1822, in E. de Selincourt, *Dorothy Wordsworth* (1933).

little food, sometimes without clothes. The lives of literary men have all too often been burdened by financial worries and follies, but it is impossible to read a detailed account of this second part of De Quincey's life without feeling that there was never one more harassed, more pitilessly borne down by adversity and confusion.

In the last few years of his life, he was more at peace. His daughters took over the management of his affairs, his position as a writer was assured, and he was largely freed from the struggle to write day by day for his living. In 1850, he began to bring together his scattered papers into a collected edition, re-writing and adding much. He died in 1859, seventy-five years of age. Whatever opium had done for him, it had not much shortened his life.

II

In a *Diary* kept in 1803, De Quincey had reviewed the literary projects of his boyhood. 'I have always intended of course', he wrote, 'that *poems* should form the corner-stone of my fame', and he gave a list of the poems, plays and tales which he had, 'at some time or other, seriously intended to execute'. So far as is known, none of them was written, and it was no great loss, for their titles suggest a dismal array of the most stilted and artificial 'romantic' themes, most of them treated 'pathetically'. At the very time when he made this list, he was growing out of these juvenile aspirations, towards the very different ambition of his idyllic years at Grasmere. The aim of his studies there, of his large library, his long leisure, was to be a great work of philosophy, which would transform education, and re-establish mathematics in England. But this too failed to get written, and when at last he set pen to paper, it was not for the sake of fame or great ambitions, but for money. The fate that befell him was one that he both feared and despised.

In 1818, he wrote to his mother: 'Like all persons who believe themselves in possession of *original* knowledge not derived from books, I was indisposed to sell my knowledge for money, and to commence trading author.'[1] But that was to be his trade, for the rest of his life.

In some ways he was unfitted for it, both by temperament and training. He lacked the self-discipline needed for the regular and punctual performance of routine tasks, and he had much of that ingenious indolence which knows how to avoid doing something arduous by elaborating the mere preparations for doing it. Rather than write the article expected of him, he would often compose a letter of explanation of his delay to the editor nearly as long as the article would have been, and quite as elaborate. Coleridge once described his turn of mind, rather unkindly but not inaccurately, as 'anxious yet dilatory, confused over accuracy, and at once systematic and labyrinthine'.[2] When to these deficiencies of temperament there was added laudanum, it is hard to imagine a man less fitted to drive the trade of writer for periodicals. Yet for thirty years De Quincey drove this trade with outstanding success. The editors put up with his unpunctuality, his dreadfully elaborate excuses for it: or at least, when one editor could bear it no longer, there was always another to take him on. For though his manner of driving his trade was outrageously unbusinesslike, he was extremely good at it. To get an article out of him might cost ten times the trouble, but when it came it might be ten times as good as another's. The qualities of his mind and style were far above those usually found in writers for periodicals, and it was only because of the defects in his temperament that he was brought down to their level. The dilettantism which had kept him reading through the ambitious years of his youth, always preparing to write, never writing, now became an asset. He had a vast

[1] A. H. Japp, *De Quincey Memorials* (1891), Vol. II, p. 114.
[2] *Letters from the Lake Poets to D. Stuart*, ed. E. H. Coleridge (1889), p. 155.

store of material, of all kinds, and a memory so tenacious that even when the need to hide from his creditors severed him from his library—as it often did—he could draw on it freely and effectively. His writing, in fact, was entirely of a piece with the whole odd pattern of his life.

It was also lucky, though perhaps it never occurred to him to think so, that he lived at a time when there was a vigorous demand for periodical writing of high quality. The great periodical magazines which had begun a century earlier were then at the height of their development, and enjoyed the support of a fairly large body of intelligent readers. A generation later, they were already in their decline, in the process of being supplanted by cheaper competitors with wider circulations and lower standards. In that last age of great periodicals, De Quincey, with Lamb and Hazlitt, enjoyed the opportunity of continuing the tradition of essay-writing which had come down to them from Addison, Johnson and Goldsmith. Between them, they made fine and varied use of it.

In range of subject, De Quincey far surpassed Lamb and Hazlitt. To read his collected essays, even today, would be a liberal education of remarkable comprehensiveness. For it would include Greek literature and philosophy, much Roman history, German literature and philosophy, modern history and literature, politics and economics; even mathematics would not be wholly absent, for in his writings on economics he made some use of mathematical arguments and illustrations, along with others—such as the factors determining the price of a rhinoceros in the seventeenth century, or of a musical snuff-box on a steamboat on Lake Eyrie, entirely typical of his taste for oddities. This education, however, would be in many respects a little out-of-date. A century of scholarship, of philosophy, and of economic speculation has turned many of his essays into period pieces, of no more than historic interest. What has survived is a smaller body of writing, not very different from that of Lamb and Hazlitt: some literary criticism and biography, records of people and events he had known at first hand, and above all, autobiography. To-day, in fact, he is most readable in those writings which most involved his own experience. And it was in these that his literary achievement was the greatest.

III

De Quincey's literary criticism differs from that of Lamb and Hazlitt in that it was only fitfully directed upon the actual works, the writings themselves. He wrote nothing like Lamb's essays on the Elizabethans, or Hazlitt's lectures on Shakespeare and his studies of contemporary writers in *The Spirit of the Age*. There is but one Shakespearean study, 'On the Knocking at the Gate of Macbeth', remarkable in its way, but brief and restricted in scope. There is one long essay 'On Milton', two on Pope, 'The Poetry of Pope' and 'Lord Carlisle on Pope', and nothing else substantial on any of our older writers. There are striking and illuminating observations in all these essays, but in all of them also a tendency to slide away into digressions, often attempting, rather in the manner of Coleridge, large philosophic generalizations about the principles of literature and criticism.

In his writings on contemporaries, his tendency was to slide away from their actual work, but in another direction, into the details of their personalities and lives. Of this, the outstanding example is his long series of essays on Wordsworth and Coleridge, and the other writers of the Lake school.[1] Only one of them, 'On Wordsworth's Poetry', even tries to deal with the poetry as such, and on the whole it fails to make clear why he had been so swiftly carried away by it as a boy. All the rest are mainly studies in personalities

[1] The dozen or so essays in this group are often collected under the title *Recollections of the Lake Poets*, as in the edition by E. Sackville-West (1948).

and biographies, even 'William Wordsworth,' in which he draws upon his preview of *The Prelude* in manuscript only for information about the life, never for criticism of the poetry. One is left with a sense of opportunity missed, a revelation never made concerning the kind of impact made by the poetry on one of its earliest disciples. On the other hand, the impulse which carried De Quincey towards biography was also valuable to us, and entirely natural to him. Not only had he lived in intimate friendship with his subjects, but he was also a gifted observer of human beings, of their appearances, manners, conduct, and—a rarer gift— of those traits which are revealed in their bodily postures and gestures. For example, he records that:

the total effect of Wordsworth's person was always worst in a state of motion . . . This was not always perceptible, and in part depended (I believe) upon the position of the arms; when either of these happened (as was very customary) to be inserted into the unbuttoned waistcoat, his walk had a wry or twisted appearance; and not appearance only— for I have known it, by slow degrees, to edge his companion from the middle to the side of the highroad. Meantime, his face—that was one which would have made amends for greater defects of figure.

Of Dorothy Wordsworth, he wrote with the same un-flattering but revealing perception:

Her manner was warm and even ardent; her sensibility seemed consti-tutionally deep; and some subtle fire of impassioned intellect apparently burned within her, which, being alternately pushed forward into a conspicuous expression by the irrepressible instincts of her temperament, and then immediately checked, in obedience to the decorum of her age and sex . . . gave to her whole demeanour, and to her conversation, an air of embarrassment, and even of self-conflict, that was almost distres-sing to witness.

It is not surprising that observations of such penetration and candour, published while their subjects were still living, should have given some offence. But there is little doubt that they are true in themselves, and they were not made

entirely for their own sake; they are aspects of the larger
picture which De Quincey built up of the remarkable
relationship between Wordsworth and his sister, and of the
special influence she had exercised on his work. This
opportunity, of observing the Wordsworth circle from
within, was certainly not missed, but recorded with perception and often with astringent objectivity.

There are similar compensations in his digressions into
the philosophy of literary art. True, they divert him from
the actual writings of Shakespeare, Milton, Pope and the
rest, but they have their own interest, being rarely less than
ingenious, and sometimes illuminating. A few, moreover,
serve to throw light on his own experience of writing.
Perhaps the best known of them is a distinction between
'the literature of knowledge' and 'the literature of power'.
It had been suggested to him in conversation by Wordsworth, but he made it his own by elaborating it over a long
period of years. It appears first in 'Letters to a Young Man',
published in 1828, and again as an extensive digression in
'The Poetry of Pope', published in 1848. The essential
difference is that the function of 'the literature of knowledge'
is to teach, to convey information, while that of 'the literature of power' is to move, to expand and exercise the
reader's 'latent capacity of sympathy with the infinite'.
From this follows a characteristic difference between the
two kinds of writing in their capacity for survival:

Hence the pre-eminency over all authors that merely *teach* of the meanest
that *moves*, or that teaches, if at all, indirectly *by* moving. The very
highest work that has ever existed in the Literature of Knowledge is
but a *provisional* work . . . Let its teaching be even partially revised, let it
be but expanded, nay, even let its teaching be but placed in a better order,
and instantly it is superseded. Whereas the feeblest works in the
Literature of Power, surviving at all, survive as finished and unalterable
among men.

The fate of De Quincey's own writings is enough to
illustrate this principle, and to confirm its general accuracy.

Whenever he wrote to instruct, whenever his subject lay mainly in the field of erudition, he has been superseded; but whenever his material was taken from his own experience, from what he had seen and lived through for himself, his writing has retained a life and power of its own.

Another of his theories about the nature of literature was concerned with 'rhetoric', of which the conception, set out in a treatise entitled 'Rhetoric' in 1828, was so eccentrically personal that it can only have been an expression of his own experience of literary creation. He rejected several accepted notions of rhetoric: it was not, for example, the mere addition of ornament to plain matter, nor was it the art of persuasion by sophistry, nor again identical with highly emotive utterance. His own definition was based upon a distinction between two opposing conditions in which any subject might exist. Much might be known about it, and with certainty; and in this condition, it would leave no scope for rhetoric. On the other hand, fixed and certain knowledge about it might be lacking, so that consideration of it must necessarily move among mere guesses and the weighing of probabilities; and in this case, the art of rhetoric might legitimately be used in swaying belief to one side or the other. He himself never suggested, perhaps never consciously realized, how nearly this view of the function of rhetoric coincided with his definition of 'the literature of power'. The consistency of his thinking depended much more upon the unconscious similarities of his insights and intuitions than upon his perception of logical relations between them. But it is clear that for him, rhetoric, like 'power', was conceived as the antithesis of fixed and certain knowledge; its sphere of operation was the same as that of literary 'power', and its function was to exercise and expand latent capacities of the mind. Two descriptions of rhetoric given in the essay show more concretely how he conceived its mode of operation. In one, he says that it is 'to hang upon one's own thoughts as an object of conscious interest, to play with them, to watch and pursue them through a maze of inversions, evolutions, and harlequin changes'. In the second, he points to the absence of true rhetoric in French prose-writers, for 'there is no eddying about their own thoughts; no motion of fancy self-sustained from its own activities; no flux and reflux of thought, half meditative, half capricious'. Of however slender use these definitions and descriptions of rhetoric may be in general, they could hardly be bettered as characterizations of one outstanding quality in De Quincey's own writing. Those parts of it which remain the most readable, which have the 'power' to survive, are precisely those in which his mind gave itself up to this free imaginative play. Some aspect of his subject, or often some digression which it suggested to him, was picked up and carried on in the 'flux and reflux of thought, half meditative, half capricious', and what he had begun as forced labour came to life under his hand.

The third of his more notable contributions to literary theory was at once the most original, and the one most nearly related with his own writing. It was a close concern with the special qualities of prose and the technique of writing it. This is a subject not very fully treated by most theorists of literature, partly, no doubt, because they have usually ranked prose so far below verse as to make it beneath the dignity of their notice, but also perhaps because the structural aspects of prose are more fluid and complex than those of verse, and so more difficult to discuss. De Quincey forcefully corrects both errors in 'Philosophy of Herodotus' (Masson, Vol. VI, p. 100):

if prose were simply the negation of verse, were it the fact that prose had no separate laws of its own, but that to be a composer of prose meant only his privilege of being inartificial, his dispensation from the restraints of metre, then, indeed, it would have been a slight nominal honour to have been the Father of Prose. But this is ignorance, though a pretty common ignorance. To walk well it is not enough that a man abstain from dancing. Walking has rules of its own the more difficult to perceive or to practise as they are less broadly prononcés. To forbear

singing is not, therefore, to speak well or to read well: each of which
offices rests upon a separate art of its own. Numerous laws of transition,
connexion, preparation, are different for a writer in verse and a writer
in prose. Each mode of composition is a great art; well executed, it is the
highest and most difficult of arts.

Scattered liberally through his essays are reflections on these
'laws' of prose, not only in English, but in Latin, Greek,
French and German. He wrote on diction, the 'choice of
words', and his comments on the functions of Romance
and Teutonic words in English, especially in the third
'Oxford' paper and 'The Poetry of Wordsworth', have
hardly been bettered since. But it was above all with what
might be called the prosody of prose that he concerned
himself, and some of his most perceptive and original
observations are on the inner harmonies of sentence-
structure, such as this in the third 'Oxford' paper (Masson,
Vol. II, p. 65):

The two capital secrets in the art of prose composition are these: 1st,
The philosophy of transition and connection, or the art by which one
step in an evolution of thought is made to arise out of another: all fluent
and effective composition depends on the *connections;* 2ndly, The way
in which sentences are made to modify each other; for the most powerful effects in written eloquence arise out of this reverberation, as it were,
from each other in a rapid succession of sentences . . .

It is worth remarking again the consistency of his intuitions:
this notion of 'reverberation' between sentences looks very
like a structural aspect of that 'flux and reflux of thought'
which was at the heart of his special definition of rhetoric.
And in his comments on the style of his contemporaries,
his more abstract doctrines on prose are applied with the
same kind of consistency to concrete cases. Thus, in 'Charles
Lamb' (Masson, Vol. V, pp. 231, 235):

. . . Hazlitt was not eloquent, because he was discontinuous. No man can
be eloquent whose thoughts are abrupt, insulated, capricious, and (to
borrow an impressive word from Coleridge) non-sequacious. Eloquence

resides not in separate or fractional ideas, but in the relations of manifold ideas, and in the mode of their evolution from each other. It is not indeed enough that the ideas should be many, and their relations coherent; the main condition lies in the *key* of the evolution, in the *law* of the succession.

In Lamb's prose, he found some great merits, but also this characteristic defect:

. . . Lamb had no sense of the rhythmical in prose compositions. Rhythmus, or pomp of cadence, or sonorous ascent of clauses, in the structure of sentences, were effects of art as much thrown away upon *him* as the voice of the charmer upon the deaf adder. We ourselves, occupying the very station of polar opposition to that of Lamb,—being as morbidly, perhaps, in the one excess as he in the other, naturally detected this omission in Lamb's nature at an early stage of our acquaintance.

The cause of this deficiency in Lamb, he insisted, was his lack of any response to music; whereas he himself was deeply interested in it throughout his life, and to this interest certainly owed much of his feeling for phrasing and structure in prose. The terms which naturally occur to him in speaking of it are often of musical origin: 'key of the evolution', 'rhythmus, or pomp of cadence, sonorous ascent of clauses'; and in some of his descriptions of music he almost exactly reproduces his doctrines on the prosody of prose, as in the following passage, from 'On Style' (Masson, Vol. X, p. 136):

A song, an air, a tune,—that is, a short succession of notes revolving rapidly upon itself,—how could that, by possibility, offer a field of compass sufficient for the development of great musical effects? The preparation pregnant with the future; the remote correspondence; the questions, as it were, which to a deep musical sense are asked in one passage, and answered in another; the iteration and ingemination of a given effect, moving through subtle variations that sometimes disguise the theme, sometimes fitfully reveal it, sometimes throw it out tumultuously to the blaze of daylight: these and ten thousand forms of self-conflicting musical passion, what room could they find, what opening, what utterance in so limited a field as an air or song?

The kind of prose which emerged from this sense of musical structure and almost symphonic complexity was specially fitted to be the instrument of De Quincey's most powerful autobiographical writings, in *The Confessions* and *Suspiria de Profundis*. Indeed no other kind would have served his purposes there, in a genre for which, in his general introduction to the collected edition of his works in 1858, he modestly claimed originality for himself, under the title of 'impassioned prose'. But the same virtues were capable of more supple and rapid effects when they were needed. His narrative prose is also admirably swift and effective, when employed on a suitable subject. It is seen at its worst in his fiction, for there he was haunted by a crazy admiration for the most outrageous kind of German romantic writing, the results of which can be seen by the curious in his *Klosterheim*. But it is at its best in parts of *The Confessions*, and in 'The English Mail-Coach', which recreates the romance of that mode of travel in its heyday, just before it was displaced by the railways. It contains one of the best descriptions in English of a fast ride by night on a crack mail-coach, and of a hair's breadth escape from a mortal accident. There are also at least two pieces of historical writing in which his narrative power is seen to the full: 'The Spanish Military Nun', and 'Revolt of the Tartars'. The first describes, at headlong pace, the adventures of a nun dressed as a soldier in a journey through South America; the second recounts the almost epic exodus of the Kalmuck Tartars from the Volga to China in 1771. In both, he had sources for the facts, in French and in German, but he used them with a free imagination, and to splendid effect. The second, especially, is a piece of his writing which has not received its due. It ends with an appalling, but magnificent description of the final massacre of the fleeing Tartars by their Bashkir pursuers in the bloodstained waters of Lake Tengis, under the very eyes of the Chinese Emperor.

It is one of the curious traits in De Quincey's character that though himself gentle to a degree, diminutive in person,

and elaborately courteous in manner, he was strangely
fascinated by scenes of violence. In 1818 he was for a short
time editor of the *Westmorland Gazette*; instead of printing
news of the day and political articles, as the proprietors
wished, he filled his columns with long reports of lurid
crimes collected from all over the country. Four years later,
he published his most famous piece of literary criticism, a
short essay 'On the Knocking at the Gate in Macbeth'. It is
as different from any other piece of Shakespearean criticism
in English as it is typical of De Quincey, for it contains a
digression, written with almost more care and interest than
the main theme, and this digression is about a specially
bloodthirsty murder. The dramatic problem, as De Quincey
posed it, was his own strong feeling that the knocking
'reflected back upon the murder a peculiar awfulness'. For
years he had been unable to find a rational cause for this
feeling, until, in 1812, the same knocking on a door in the
silence of the night had followed after a multiple murder in
London. 'The same incident', De Quincey observes, 'did
actually occur which the genius of Shakespeare had in-
vented; and all good judges, and the most eminent dilettanti,
acknowledged the felicity of Shakespeare's suggestion as
soon as it was actually realized.' Its dramatic and imaginative
function in the play, he thought, was to emphasize the
enormity and inhumanity of Duncan's murder: 'the re-
establishment of the goings-on of the world in which we
live first makes us profoundly sensible of the awful paren-
thesis that had suspended them'. In Shakespearian criticism,
this was an isolated lucky hit, so far as De Quincey was
concerned. And it remained isolated because what had
really caught his imagination was not Shakespeare and
Shakespearean interpretation, but the odd notion that there
might, after all, be an imaginative, even an artistic side to
the most brutal murders—a side which would serve to
explain to himself his own interest in them. The digression
on the London murder tumbles suddenly, accidentally
(though by a significant accident), on this idea: 'In 1812,

Mr Williams made his début on the stage of the Ratcliffe Highway, and executed those unparalleled murders which have procured for him such a brilliant and undying reputation. On which murders, by the way, I must observe that in one respect they have had an ill effect by making the connoisseur in murder very fastidious in his taste, and dissatisfied with anything that has been since done in that line.' It was this half-fanciful, but also half-serious notion of connoisseurship, dilettantism in murder, that De Quincey picked up, and made the basis of a series of three papers on 'Murder Considered as One of the Fine Arts', the first in 1827, the second in 1839, while the third was specially written in 1854 for the collected edition of his works: it was a series of accounts of actual murders, notable for their ferocity (including those of the immortal artist Williams), and it shows De Quincey's narrative power at its gloomy best.

In some ways, these strange productions anticipate the literature of crime and violence which has become so large a part of popular fiction since Poe. But De Quincey's attitude towards his own interest in such themes was far more complex. He recognized its force, but at the same time saw that it was at odds with his fastidious sense of gentleness and culture. This deep-seated duality of feeling appears in his treatment of the subject as a continual colouring or irony, almost of mock-morality, in which the moral issues are ingeniously reversed, as in the passage from the second paper on 'Murder Considered as One of the Fine Arts' (Masson, Vol. XIII, p. 56):

. . . if once a man indulges himself in murder, very soon he comes to think little of robbing, and from robbing he comes next to drinking and Sabbath-breaking, and from that to incivility and procrastination. Once begin upon his downward path, you never know where you are to stop. Many a man dated his ruin from some murder or other that perhaps he thought little of at the time.

The same half-serious, half-jesting mock-morality was elaborated into a formal defence of this new field of artistic criticism. In the first of his papers, he compared murders with large fires in respect of their artistic merits, and described an occasion when he had been taking tea with Coleridge, who was discussing Plato; news had been brought that a large building was on fire nearby, and the whole party had rushed out to see it, 'as it promised to be a conflagration of merit'. He himself had been compelled to leave before the climax, but meeting Coleridge afterwards, he had asked 'how that very promising exhibition had terminated'. 'Oh, sir', said he, 'it turned out so ill that we damned it unanimously.' This did not mean, he points out, that Coleridge was incendiary-minded, or lacking in moral feeling. 'Virtue was in no request. On the arrival of the fire-engines, morality had devolved wholly on the insurance office. This being the case, he had a right to gratify his taste. He had left his tea. Was he to have nothing in return?' From examples such as these, De Quincey elicited a novel general principle:

> Everything in this world has two handles. Murder, for instance, may be laid hold of by its moral handle (as it generally is in the pulpit, and at the Old Bailey); and *that*, I confess, is its weak side; or it may also be treated *aesthetically*, as the Germans call it—that is, in relation to good taste.

This seems to be the first use of the word 'aesthetic' in this sense in English—it is seven years earlier than the first examples given in the Oxford English Dictionary. De Quincey must certainly be credited, among his contributions to literary criticism, with having been the first to advance a theory which was to acquire great influence later in the nineteenth century, and not only in England, the theory that developed into the richer formulations of Pater and Baudelaire, and then into the vulgarized formula of 'art for art's sake'.

But this tentative and ironic aestheticism is not merely a curious fact in literary history. It is also striking evidence of the strength of the tensions within his own personality, of the strange contrast between the humdrum domesticity of his outward life, and the exotic violence of his inner world. Of this tension, the curious papers on 'Murder Considered as One of the Fine Arts' are but a minor product. Its major expression is in the *Confessions* and its continuations, for there, without the disguise of ironic humour, he tries to explore and explain, above all to himself, the destiny which had placed such a gulf between his outward and inward lives.

IV

For the more lurid implications of the term 'Opium-Eater', De Quincey was himself responsible. And he was exaggerating, no doubt for the sake of emphasis. Solid opium was at times in his possession, and on occasions he ate it. But his regular sustenance was the less sensational tincture of laudanum, on sale in every apothecary's shop and kept in the medicine cupboard of every well-run household, much as aspirin is today, as the normal remedy for all kinds of aches and pains. It was recommended for such purposes to the prudent housewife in Buchan's *Domestic Medicine*, a widely used handbook of the time, but with the solemn warning that it might be abused as well as used. Its disadvantage was notoriously that some of those who took it first as a medicine might become addicted to it as a drug, and come to depend upon it, not as a palliative for a cough or a toothache, but as a means of blunting their reactions to all the stresses and tensions of their lives. This is what had happened to Coleridge when De Quincey met him—on the first day of their acquaintance, the older man solemnly warned the younger against the drug. Later the same addiction overtook other writers, Keats and Wilkie Collins among them, and many who were not writers. But De Quincey was the only one who wrote about his addiction openly, studying it with an almost clinical detachment.

Indeed this air of scientific frankness, of a man laying his private secrets bare for the public good, was one of the ways in which he seems to have quieted his conscience and kept up his self-respect—and hoped to retain the respect of others.

His verdict on opium as a drug, and on himself as an addict, was that his personality had not been changed, morally or mentally; that his faculties and his general health had been impaired temporarily, but not irrecoverably; and that the inevitable final pains of opium were much greater than its early pleasures. There was, however, one really important discovery, one really revealing aspect of his 'case': the drug had greatly intensified the workings of some faculties, especially those of memory and of dreaming, and had enabled him to discover some laws of their operation which, without this intensification, he would never have been able to observe. In giving a careful account of them, he believed that he was saying something both true and useful not only about himself, but about the growth and structure of the human personality in general. It is in this sense that the *Confessions* deserve to be looked on as something like a prose equivalent of Wordsworth's *Prelude*. Both are intensely personal, yet objective in their mode of observation and presentation; both are attempts to reveal, by the exploration of autobiographical material, common and fundamental aspects of the human spirit; and both are perhaps easier to understand in the light of modern psychology than they were in their own day. De Quincey's is, of course, by many degrees the lesser work, more limited in its scope, less sustained, less penetrating even at its best. But it deserves to be read and judged in the light rather of this comparison than of the more lurid expectations aroused by its title.

Compared with *The Prelude*, the *Confessions* are not merely prose: they are prosaic, at any rate in their account of the outward events of De Quincey's early life. They rehearse that first crisis, the flight from Manchester Grammar School, the wanderings in Wales, and those months in London, cold and hungry, lying down at night in a bleak room lent by the agent of a money-lender, by day walking miserably through streets and parks. And here, at least, the tone rises above the prosaic, as he tells of his friendship with Ann, a girl of the streets, sixteen years old—he was seventeen himself. As two waifs in the vast friendlessness of London, they walked up and down Oxford Street, sometimes sitting on steps and under porticos, always afraid of being moved on by the watchmen. One night, he was ill from want of food, and she fetched him a stimulant which, he firmly believed, saved his life—and paid for it herself. A few days later, he left London for a few days, and when he parted from her agreed where they should meet on his return. But she was not at their meeting-place, that night nor any other:

To this hour I have never heard a syllable about her. This, amongst such troubles as most men meet with in this life, has been my heaviest affliction. If she lived, doubtless we must have been sometimes in search of each other, at the very same moment, through the mighty labyrinths of London; perhaps even within a few feet of each other—a barrier no wider, in a London street, often amounting in the end to a separation for eternity! During some years I hoped that she *did* live; and I suppose that, in the literal and unrhetorical use of the word *myriad*, I must, on my different visits to London, have looked into many myriads of female faces, in the hope of meeting Ann.[1]

After this story of his first visit to London, the tone of the narrative sinks again to the entirely prosaic, until it comes to his first experience of opium, while he was still at Oxford, but often spending vacations in London. At this stage, he found it not only a refuge against physical pain but a mental and physical stimulant. He would take it regularly on Saturday nights, and it would send him to the opera, or wandering among people and streets and faces, with

[1] *Confessions*, Masson, Vol. III, p. 375.

curiously heightened sensibilities. There is a brief glimpse of his earlier days at Grasmere with the Wordsworths, and then the statement that in 1813 he had become 'a regular and confirmed (no longer intermitting) opium-eater'. The immediate cause was illness, but this in turn had been brought about by his paroxysm of grief at the death of Kate Wordsworth, at the age of three. From this first period of deep addiction, when he was taking a daily dose of laudanum enough to have killed a hundred people not habituated to it, he was roused by the awful reaction of the drug itself, by 'the pains of opium'. The worst of its symptoms was an uncontrollable stream of fearful dreams, which tyrannized over him not only in sleep but in the whole of his waking life. And it is in the description of these dreams that De Quincey rises decisively above the prosaic, into his own unique kind of 'impassioned prose.' The style reflects his long and careful study of prose as an artistic medium, above all his sense of its analogies with music. Many years later, in the general preface written for his collected works, he pleaded 'the perilous difficulty besieging all attempts to clothe in words the visionary scenes derived from the world of dreams, where a single false note, a single word in the wrong key, ruins the whole music'. And the substance of the dreams was woven from his earlier life, from the formative experiences of his child-hood and youth:

In the early stage of the malady, the splendours of my dreams were indeed chiefly architectural; and I beheld such pomp of cities and palaces as never yet was beheld by waking eye, unless in the clouds . . . To my architecture succeeded dreams of lakes and silvery expanses of water . . . The waters gradually changed their character—from translucent lakes, shining like mirrors, they became seas and oceans. And now came a tremendous change, which, unfolding itself slowly like a scroll, through many months, promised an abiding torment; and, in fact, it never left me, though recurring more or less intermittingly. Hitherto the human face had often mixed in my dreams, but not despotically, nor with any special power of tormenting. But now that affection which

I have called the tyranny of the human face began to unfold itself.
Perhaps some part of my London life (the searching for Ann amongst
fluctuating crowds) might be answerable for this. Be that as it may, now
it was that upon the rocking waters of the ocean the human face began
to reveal itself; the sea appeared paved with innumerable faces, up-
turned to the heavens; faces, imploring, wrathful, despairing; faces that
surged upwards by thousands, by myriads, by generations; infinite was
my agitation; my mind tossed, as it seemed, upon the billowy ocean,
and weltered upon the weltering waves.[1]

The scene was an oriental one; and there also it was Easter Sunday, and
very early in the morning. And at a vast distance were visible, as a stain
upon the horizon, the domes and cupolas of a great city . . . And not a
bow-shot from me, upon a stone, shaded by Judean palms, there sat a
woman; and I looked, and it was—Ann! She fixed her eyes upon me
earnestly, and I said to her at length, 'So, then, I have found you at last.'
I waited; but she answered me not a word . . . Seventeen years ago,
when the lamp-light of mighty London fell upon her face, as for the last
time I kissed her lips . . . her eyes were streaming with tears. The tears
were now no longer seen. Sometimes she seemed altered; yet sometimes
again *not* altered; and hardly older. Her looks were tranquil, but with
unusual solemnity of expression, and I now gazed upon her with some
awe. Suddenly her countenance grew dim; and, turning to the mountains, I perceived vapours rolling between us; in a moment all had
vanished; thick darkness came on; and in the twinkling of an eye I was
far away from the mountains, and by lamp-light in London, walking
again with Ann—just as we had walked, when both children, eighteen
years before, along the endless terraces of Oxford Street.[2]

The *Confessions* end with this procession of dreams, and
with the equivocal assertion that the habit of opium had
been nearly conquered. In a sense, they were unfinished,
since the addiction was not conquered either. He was to go
further and deeper among the pains of opium, and into the
history of his own spirit. But twenty-five years passed
before the ability not only to dream but also to describe his
dreams visited him again, probably in what modern

[1] *Confessions*, Masson, Vol. III, pp. 439-41.
[2] ibid, pp. 445-6.

physicians call the period of 'withdrawal', when, after heavy addiction to a narcotic, the doses are suddenly reduced. In 1845, he resumed his *Confessions*, and thought that what he had written was 'the *ne plus ultra*, as regards the feeling and the power to express it, which I can ever hope to attain'.[1] Like so many of his projects, this continuation was not achieved completely. All that is left, and probably all that he wrote, is a series of fragments, linked by no coherent plan, but in some very significant ways deepening the self-analysis of the earlier work, and carrying the splendour of 'impassioned prose' still further.

It would be a service to his reputation, even now, to link these fragments with the original *Confessions* in such a way as to bring out the fundamental coherence of the whole sequence—a coherence not of logical structure, but of emotion and of recollection. Certainly the beginning of such a re-arrangement would be a paper written in this Indian summer of 1845, and called 'The Affliction of Child-hood' (Masson, Vol. I, pp. 35-49). In it he describes, for the first time fully, the death of his specially beloved sister Elizabeth, when he was seven years old, the sister who, more than any other human being, had given him the full security of real affection. With appalling clarity he wrote of his clandestine visit to the room where her body lay in a blaze of sunlight, and of his last kiss on her dead lips. And he goes on, in some of his most perceptive explorations of his own memories, to explain to himself why death, and above all the death of young girls, should have become inextricably woven in his mind with the images of summer, sunlight, Palestine, Jerusalem and Easter Day. It is in this entangled mass of associations that he found the reason why he should have encountered Ann in his dreams beneath Judean palms, within sight of Jerusalem. And he became aware that her figure was, for him, but another incarnation of the sister who had died when he was a child. A third incarnation of

[1] 'Letter to Professor Lushington', 1845, in H. A. Page, *Thomas De Quincey: his Life and Writings* (1877), Vol. I, p. 338.

the same image of death and the maiden was Kate Wordsworth, who had died at the age of three in 1813, and whose death had precipitated his first deep addiction to opium. In the earlier *Confessions*, there is an Easter-Day dream of the sun-drenched churchyard among the mountains where she was buried, but it needs to be rounded out by his account of his extraordinary affection for her and his paroxysm of grief at her death, published in 1840.[1] These three girls, his sister Elizabeth, the street-girl Ann, and Kate Wordsworth were woven interchangeably into his recurring dream of death and summer—'having been once roused, it never left me, and split into a thousand fantastic variations, which often suddenly re-combined, locked back into startling unity, and restored the original dream'.[2] Some of the most singular and lovely of these variations are in the new fragments, to which he gave the title *Suspiria de Profundis*. Perhaps the best-known of all his pieces of 'impassioned prose' is the triptych of three ambiguously allegorical female figures, shadowily representing the modes of grief in despair and madness. Here is one of them:

The second Sister is called *Mater Suspiriorum*, Our Lady of Sighs. She never scales the clouds, nor walks abroad upon the winds. She wears no diadem. And her eyes, if they were ever seen, would be neither sweet nor subtle; no man could read their story; they would be found filled with perishing dreams, and with wrecks of forgotten delirium. But she raises not her eyes . . . She weeps not. She groans not. But she sighs inaudibly at intervals. Her sister, Madonna, is oftentimes stormy and frantic, raging in the highest against heaven, and demanding back her darlings. But Our Lady of Sighs never clamours, never defies, dreams not of rebellious aspirations. She is humble to abjectness. Hers is the meekness that belongs to the hopeless. Murmur she may, but it is in her sleep. Whisper she may, but it is to herself in the twilight. Mutter she does at times, but it is in solitary places that are desolate as she is desolate, in ruined cities, and when the sun has gone down to his rest.[3]

---

[1] Masson, Vol. II, pp. 440–5.
[2] *Confessions*, Masson, Vol. III, p. 444.
[3] 'Levana and Our Lady of Sorrows', Masson, Vol. XIII, p. 366.

It would be hard to find a better example of what De Quincey himself described as 'the capital secrets' of prose, for here it is by the connexions between the sentences, and the 'reverberations' between them that the effect is attained. It is, indeed, a compressed demonstration of the devices by which the implied intonation of the speaking voice may be controlled. There is inversion of the usual order—'murmur she may'; a subtle use of parallelism and antitheses; and above all, in the last three sentences, a repetition of the same basic pattern, but with a lengthening of the variations so that they lead with musical inevitability to the final cadence. The whole effect is one rare in English prose—and perhaps not entirely to the taste of most readers and writers of English prose. In French, it can be savoured more frankly, and in Baudelaire's magnificent version of it, the strict harmony of its sentence-structure emerges even more firmly than in the original.[1]

A few more dream-fragments in his highest strain are to be found in 'The English Mail-Coach', another product of the second period of his creative dreams. Here is one from the 'Dream-Fugue', which represents his last attempt to lift prose to the level of music, and which gives another variation of his endless dream of dying girls, more purely, less rhetorically, than in the *Suspiria*:

Sweet funeral bells from some incalculable distance, wailing over the dead that die before the dawn, awakened me as I slept in a boat moored to some familiar shore. The morning twilight even then was breaking; and, by the dusky revelations which it spread, I saw a girl, adorned with a garland of white roses about her head for some great festival, running along the solitary strand in extremity of haste. Her running was the running of panic; and often she looked back as to some dreadful enemy in the rear. But, when I leaped ashore, and followed on her steps to warn her of a peril in front, alas! from me she fled as from another peril, and vainly I shouted to her of quicksands that lay ahead.

[1] De Quincey's influence upon French literature was considerably greater than upon English. Musset translated the *Confessions* in 1828, and Balzac, Gautier and Baudelaire made more or less extensive use of the images in them.

Faster and faster she ran; round a promontory of rocks she wheeled out
of sight; in an instant I also wheeled round it, but only to see the
treacherous sands gathering above her head. Already her person was
buried; only the fair young head and the diadem of white roses above it
were still visible to the pitying heavens; and, last of all, was visible one
white marble arm.[1]

For writing in this mode, De Quincey is often enjoyed,
sometimes praised—and rightly, for there is nothing quite
like it in English. But he is also criticized for it, on the ground
that it is over-elaborate, 'Mandarin' prose. So far as this
may be a matter of taste, there is no point in disputing it;
but to whatever extent it may rest on preconceptions of the
nature of language and of literature, it is open to argument.
First, it should be remembered that modern linguistics lays
stress upon the many 'registers' of a single language, and
happens to describe them by a musical metaphor from one
of De Quincey's favourite instruments, the organ, in which
a register is a set of stops producing the same quality of
sound, in the same way. There are on the organ itself
registers which need to be used with discretion; but so used,
they are no less effective, no less essential than others. And
in prose there are kinds of registration which are only
needed, only artistically justified, for a few special purposes;
but for those purposes they are irreplaceable. De Quincey's
own plea, of the rarity and difficulty of transcribing dreams,
carries real weight. The dream rarely offers determinate
shapes, hard outlines and clear-cut detail; what overwhelms
in it is the atmosphere, the immense suggestion of emotion.
And for the rendering of this shadowy essence, De Quincey's
prose was an admirable, an indispensable medium.

Secondly, it must not be forgotten that he was not
concerned with dream writing for its own sake. It was no
more, and no less, than the special material on which he
founded his study of the growth of the human spirit. And
just as it is possible—and very common—for Wordsworth

[1] 'The English Mail-Coach', Masson, Vol. XIII, p. 321.

to be read for the sake of the descriptions, while their purpose is nearly overlooked, so De Quincey is too often read for the sake of his purpler passages, without regard for the explorations of which they are merely a part. No doubt the reason is that his passages of reflection and analysis, like Wordsworth's occasional philosophic comments, are more soberly written, less superficially attractive and striking than the material on which they rest. But for him they were the justification of his enterprise, and not in any narrowly artistic sense. In the *Confessions* there are some fine passages on memory, above all the memory of childhood, and its formative effect on the human personality; in its continuation, the *Suspiria*, there are finer still, for they gain by his deeper understanding of himself, his more sensitive evocation of the experiences which had shaped his dreams, and himself. In 'The Affliction of Childhood', for example, there is this profound perception:

Far more of our deepest thoughts and feelings pass to us through perplexed combinations of concrete objects, pass to us as *involutes* (if I may coin that word) in compound experiences incapable of being disentangled, than ever reach us *directly*, and in their own abstract shapes.

Wordsworth himself continually exemplified this vital aspect of human experience, but never defined it quite so clearly. And in this passage on his own chosen ground, the theory of dreams, De Quincey shows not only that he has something of importance to report, but also that his prose, even at its most elaborate, was no less capable of precise exposition than of visionary description: and it was so because his 'fine writing' depended, not on a curious choice of words, but upon the firm and supple structure of sentences musically moulded, unfolding a theme and its development to the final cadence with that special sureness of phrasing which links each moment of melody with the whole magnificent composition:

... countless are the mysterious handwritings of grief or joy which have inscribed themselves successively upon the palimpsest of your brain; and, like the annual leaves of aboriginal forests, or the undissolving snows on the Himalaya, or light falling upon light, the endless strata have covered up each other in forgetfulness. But by the hour of death, but by fever, but by the searchings of opium, all these can revive in strength. They are not dead, but sleeping. In the illustration imagined by myself from the case of some individual palimpsest, the Grecian tragedy had seemed to be displaced, but was *not* displaced, by the monkish legend; and the monkish legend had seemed to be displaced, but was *not* displaced, by the knightly romance. In some potent convulsion of the system, all wheels back into its earliest elementary stage. The bewildering romance, light tarnished with darkness, the semi-fabulous legend, truth celestial mixed with human falsehoods, these fade even of themselves as life advances. The romance has perished that the young man adored; the legend has gone that deluded the boy; but the deep, deep tragedies of infancy, as when the child's hands were unlinked for ever from his mother's neck, or his lips for ever from his sister's kisses, these remain lurking below all, and these lurk to the last. Alchemy there is none of passion or disease that can scorch away these immortal impresses . . .[1]

His daughter described the moment of De Quincey's death thus: 'suddenly we saw him throw up his arms, which to the last retained their strength, and say distinctly, and as if in great surprise, "Sister! sister! sister!" The loud breathing became slower and slower, and as the world of Edinburgh awoke to busy work and life, all that was mortal of my father fell asleep for ever.' He was a man, then, who had come to know himself, and, without rhetoric, what for him would indeed lurk to the last.

[1] 'The Palimpsest of the Human Brain', in *Suspiria de Profundis*, Masson, Vol. XIII, pp. 348-9.

THOMAS DE QUINCEY

A Select Bibliography

(Place of publication London, unless stated otherwise)

Bibliography:

THOMAS DE QUINCEY: A Bibliography based upon the De Quincey collection in the Moss Side Library [Manchester], by J. A. Green; Manchester (1908).

'The Canon of De Quincey's Writings, with some references to his unidentified articles', by W. E. A. Axon, *Transactions of the Royal Society of Literature*, XXXII, 1912.

Collected Works:

DE QUINCEY'S WRITINGS, ed. J. T. Fields, 22 vols; Boston (1851-9)
—unrevised text. Reprinted as Author's Library Edition, Boston, 1878.

SELECTIONS GRAVE AND GAY FROM WRITINGS, PUBLISHED AND UN-PUBLISHED, OF THOMAS DE QUINCEY, REVISED AND ARRANGED BY HIMSELF, 14 vols; Edinburgh (1853-60)
—'Author's Collected Edition', of his previously published writings, enlarged, recast and revised.

THE COLLECTED WRITINGS, ed., with an Inttroduction and Notes, by D. Masson, 14 vols; Edinburgh (1889-90)
—the standard edition; several times reprinted.

THE POSTHUMOUS WORKS, ed. from the original MSS with an Introduction and Notes by A. H. Japp, 2 vols (1891-3).

Selected Works:

SELECT ESSAYS, ed. D. Masson, 2 vols; Edinburgh (1888).

ESSAYS. With an Introduction by C. Whibley (1903).

DE QUINCEY'S LITERARY CRITICISM, ed. with an Introduction by H. Darbishire (1909).

THE ENGLISH MAIL-COACH AND OTHER ESSAYS (1912)
—Everyman's Library edition.

THE ECSTASIES OF THOMAS DE QUINCEY, chosen by T. Burke (1928).

SELECTIONS FROM DE QUINCEY, ed. A. H. R. Ball (1932).

SELECTED WRITINGS OF THOMAS DE QUINCEY, ed. P. Van D. Stern; New York (1937).

RECOLLECTIONS OF THE LAKE POETS, ed. with an Introduction by E. Sackville-West (1948).

CONFESSIONS OF AN ENGLISH OPIUM-EATER, TOGETHER WITH SELECTIONS FROM THE AUTOBIOGRAPHY OF THOMAS DE QUINCEY, ed. with an Introduction by E. Sackville-West (1950).

THOMAS DE QUINCEY, ed. B. Dobrée (1965).

Separate Works:

CONFESSIONS OF AN ENGLISH OPIUM EATER (1822)
—published anonymously; revised, 1823; much enlarged, 1856; Everyman's Library, 1907; ed. G. Saintsbury, 1927. French translations by Musset, 1828, and Baudelaire, 1860.

KLOSTERHEIM; OR, THE MASQUE; Edinburgh (1832).

THE LOGIC OF POLITICAL ECONOMY; Edinburgh (1844).

CHINA. A revised reprint of articles from *Titan*, with prefaces and additions; Edinburgh (1857).

THE WILDER HOPE: Essays on future punishment, with a paper on the supposed scriptural expression for eternity (1890).

NEW ESSAYS BY DE QUINCEY: His contributions to the *Edinburgh Saturday Post* and the *Edinburgh Evening Post*, 1827-8, ed. S. M. Tave; Princeton (1966)
—articles attributed with varying degrees of certainty to De Quincey.
Note: Among the many periodicals to which De Quincey contributed were the *Westmorland Gazette* (1818-19); the *London Magazine* (1821-5); *Blackwood's Magazine* (1826-8, 1830-4, 1837-45, 1849); *Tait's Magazine* (1833-41, 1845-8, 1851); *Hogg's Instructor* (1850-3); and *Titan* (1856-7).

Letters and Diaries:

DE QUINCEY MEMORIALS, ed. A. H. Japp, 2 vols (1891)
—'Letters and other Records, with communications from Coleridge, the Wordsworths . . .'

A DIARY OF THOMAS DE QUINCEY, 1803, ed. H. A. Eaton (1928).

DE QUINCEY AT WORK: As seen in one hundred and thirty new and newly edited letters, ed. W. H. Bonner; Buffalo (1936).

UNPUBLISHED LETTERS OF THOMAS DE QUINCEY AND ELIZABETH BARRETT BROWNING, ed. S. Musgrove; Auckland (1954)
—from the originals in the Grey Collection, Auckland Public Library.

Biography and Criticism:

THOMAS DE QUINCEY: His Life and Writings, by 'H. A. Page' [*pseud.* A. H. Japp] 2 vols (1877)
—revised and enlarged, 1890.

REMINISCENCES, by T. Carlyle, ed. J. A. Froude, 2 vols (1881).

DE QUINCEY, by D. Masson (1881)
—in the 'English Men of Letters' series.

PERSONAL RECOLLECTIONS OF THOMAS DE QUINCEY, by J. R. Findlay; Edinburgh (1886).

DE QUINCEY AND HIS FRIENDS: Personal recollections, souvenirs and anecdotes, by J. Hogg (1895).

BAUDELAIRE ET DE QUINCEY, by G. T. Clapton; Paris (1931).

THE COMMON READER, by V. Woolf. 2nd series (1932)
—contains 'De Quincey's Autobiography'.

THE MILK OF PARADISE: The effect of opium visions on the works of De Quincey, Crabbe, Francis Thompson and Coleridge, by M. H. Abrams; Cambridge, Mass. (1934).

DE QUINCEY, by M. Elwin (1935).

THOMAS DE QUINCEY: A Biography, by H. A. Eaton; Oxford (1936).

A FLAME IN SUNLIGHT: The Life and Work of Thomas de Quincey, by E. Sackville-West (1936).

THOMAS DE QUINCEY, MYSTIQUE ET SYMBOLISTE, by G-A. Astre; Paris (1937).

DE QUINCEY: A Portrait, by J. C. Metcalf; Cambridge, Mass. (1940).

THOMAS DE QUINCEY'S THEORY OF LITERATURE, by S. K. Proctor; Ann Arbor (1943).

THOMAS DE QUINCEY, LITERARY CRITIC: His method and achievement, by J. E. Jordan; Berkeley & Los Angeles (1952).

'De Quincey as Literary Critic' by Clifford Leech, *A Review of English Literature*, II, 1, January 1960.

'De Quincey on "The Knocking at the Gate" ' by Geoffrey Carnall, *A Review of English Literature*, II, i, January 1960.

DE QUINCEY TO WORDSWORTH: A Biography of a relationship, by J. E. Jordan; Berkeley & Los Angeles (1962).

THOMAS DE QUINCEY: La vie—l'homme—l'œuvre, by F. Moreux; Paris (1964).

THE MINE AND THE MINT: Sources for the writings of Thomas De Quincey, by A. Goldman; Carbondale, Edwardsville (1965).

WRITERS AND THEIR WORK

CARLYLE: David Gascoyne
LEWIS CARROLL: Derek Hudson
COLERIDGE: Kathleen Raine
CREEVEY & GREVILLE: J. Richardson
DE QUINCEY: Hugh Sykes Davies
DICKENS: K. J. Fielding
  EARLY NOVELS: T. Blount
  LATER NOVELS: B. Hardy
DISRAELI: Paul Bloomfield
GEORGE ELIOT: Lettice Cooper
FERRIER & GALT: W. M. Parker
FITZGERALD: Joanna Richardson
ELIZABETH GASKELL: Miriam Allott
GISSING: A. C. Ward
THOMAS HARDY: R. A. Scott-James
              and C. Day Lewis
HAZLITT: J. B. Priestley
HOOD: Laurence Brander
G. M. HOPKINS: Geoffrey Grigson
T. H. HUXLEY: William Irvine
KEATS: Edmund Blunden
LAMB: Edmund Blunden
LANDOR: G. Rostrevor Hamilton
EDWARD LEAR: Joanna Richardson
MACAULAY: G. R. Potter
MEREDITH: Phyllis Bartlett
JOHN STUART MILL: M. Cranston
WILLIAM MORRIS: P. Henderson
NEWMAN: J. M. Cameron
PATER: Ian Fletcher
PEACOCK: J. I. M. Stewart
ROSSETTI: Oswald Doughty
CHRISTINA ROSSETTI: G. Battiscombe
RUSKIN: Peter Quennell
SIR WALTER SCOTT: Ian Jack
SHELLEY: G. M. Matthews
SOUTHEY: Geoffrey Carnall
LESLIE STEPHEN: Phyllis Grosskurth
R. L. STEVENSON: G. B. Stern
SWINBURNE: H. J. C. Grierson
TENNYSON: B. C. Southam
THACKERAY: Laurence Brander
FRANCIS THOMPSON: P. Butter
TROLLOPE: Hugh Sykes Davies
OSCAR WILDE: James Laver
WORDSWORTH: Helen Darbishire

Twentieth Century:
CHINUA ACHEBE: A. Ravenscroft
W. H. AUDEN: Richard Hoggart
HILAIRE BELLOC: Renée Haynes
ARNOLD BENNETT: F. Swinnerton
EDMUND BLUNDEN: Alec M. Hardie
ROBERT BRIDGES: J. Sparrow
ANTHONY BURGESS: Carol M. Dix
ROY CAMPBELL: David Wright
JOYCE CARY: Walter Allen
G. K. CHESTERTON: C. Hollis
WINSTON CHURCHILL: John Connell

R. G. COLLINGWOOD: E. W. F. Tomlin
I. COMPTON-BURNETT:
              R. Glynn Grylls
JOSEPH CONRAD: Oliver Warner
WALTER DE LA MARE: K. Hopkins
NORMAN DOUGLAS: Ian Greenlees
LAWRENCE DURRELL: G. S. Fraser
T. S. ELIOT: M. C. Bradbrook
FIRBANK & BETJEMAN: J. Brooke
FORD MADOX FORD: Kenneth Young
E. M. FORSTER: Rex Warner
CHRISTOPHER FRY: Derek Stanford
JOHN GALSWORTHY: R. H. Mottram
WM. GOLDING: Clive Pemberton
ROBERT GRAVES: M. Seymour-Smith
GRAHAM GREENE: Francis Wyndham
L. P. HARTLEY: Paul Bloomfield
A. E. HOUSMAN: Ian Scott-Kilvert
ALDOUS HUXLEY: Jocelyn Brooke
HENRY JAMES: Michael Swan
PAMELA HANSFORD JOHNSON:
              Isabel Quigly
JAMES JOYCE: J. I. M. Stewart
RUDYARD KIPLING: Bonamy Dobrée
D. H. LAWRENCE: Kenneth Young
C. DAY LEWIS: Clifford Dyment
WYNDHAM LEWIS: E. W. F. Tomlin
COMPTON MACKENZIE: K. Young
LOUIS MACNEICE: John Press
KATHERINE MANSFIELD: Ian Gordon
JOHN MASEFIELD: L. A. G. Strong
SOMERSET MAUGHAM: J. Brophy
GEORGE MOORE: A. Norman Jeffares
J. MIDDLETON MURRY: Philip Mairet
R. K. NARAYAN: William Walsh
SEAN O'CASEY: W. A. Armstrong
GEORGE ORWELL: Tom Hopkinson
JOHN OSBORNE: Simon Trussler
HAROLD PINTER: John Russell Taylor
POETS OF 1939-45 WAR: R. N. Currey
ANTHONY POWELL: Bernard Bergonzi
POWYS BROTHERS: R. C. Churchill
J. B. PRIESTLEY: Ivor Brown
HERBERT READ: Francis Berry
FOUR REALIST NOVELISTS: V. Brome
BERNARD SHAW: A. C. Ward
EDITH SITWELL: John Lehmann
KENNETH SLESSOR: C. Semmler
C. P. SNOW: William Cooper
SYNGE & LADY GREGORY: E. Coxhead
DYLAN THOMAS: G. S. Fraser
G. M. TREVELYAN: J. H. Plumb
WAR POETS: 1914-18: E. Blunden
EVELYN WAUGH: Christopher Hollis
H. G. WELLS: Montgomery Belgion
PATRICK WHITE: R. F. Brissenden
ANGUS WILSON: K. W. Gransden
VIRGINIA WOOLF: B. Blackstone
W. B. YEATS: G. S. Fraser